M... Through Menopause

Motorcycles Not Required... Only Hot Flashes

Jean Cheeley • Dianne Grabowski

Illustrated by Jean Cheeley

Live your adventure!
Dianne

Jorjeanna Press

ISBN 0-9644484-0-8

Library of Congress Catalog Number: 2003102497

Book design and typesetting: Mori Studio
Cover design: Jean Cheeley

Printed in the United States of America

First Printing: March 2003

06 05 04 03 6 5 4 3 2 1

Jorjeanna Press

To order, visit *www.geocities.com/motorcyclingthroughmenopause*

To our Moms

(the best Moms in the world)

who gave us the ability

to laugh at ourselves

and look for the fun in life

Table of Contents

Acknowledgements

We would like to thank our husbands, Dennis and Don, for starting us on the road to new adventures, our friends for sharing their menopausal life experiences with us, and our children for supporting our ideas in writing this book. Most of all, we would like to thank Dianne's son, Darren Augustine, for adding humor and expertise with his writing talents.

We can't forget to thank our editor, Barbara Winter, for her editing skills and for her great sense of humor as she encouraged us along the way.

Introduction

This is not intended to be a middle-aged woman's version of *Zen and the Art of Motorcycle Maintenance,* but rather a light-hearted attempt at tying a motorcycle trip through Canada and the Western United States to a philosophy of life for women who are apprehensive about reaching the age of menopause.

The problem with reaching menopause is that our society has adopted an erroneous myth that mistakes and misidentifies this season for women. American culture suggests that there is a rapid transition from the spring season of raising children, directly to the winter season of old age and immobility.

We are suggesting that menopause is the beginning of an autumn season, a season of freedom from parenting responsibilities, to be relished and enjoyed like the warm breeze of a fall day. How distressing it would be for a tree to drop its leaves on the last day of summer!

When we first reach this part of life's passage—the infamous stage known as Middle Age—we begin to develop some reservations, harbor some doubts, and face new issues and ideas about our roles in life. The two of us, lifelong friends thought of by others as conservative types, thought we needed to try something uncharacteristic of our own lives and embark on a new adventure—something that might ripple the placid waters of the lives into which we had grown accustomed. We began thinking motorcycling just might be the adventure we were looking for.

For us, both schoolteachers, motorcycling was definitely outside of our comfort zone; however, together we were excited to take the risk and try something new. Along the way, throughout the days and weeks of motorcycling, we would encounter for the first time many new and exciting adventures. We had traveled often before, but never by motorcycle. Our age, along with our inexperience on motorcycles, provided us with new insights into this stage of life resulting in a new vision of hope and excitement. What we discovered went far beyond our expectations, inspired us to share our thoughts, and gave us the courage to write this book.

Come along and join the ride.

The Adventure Unfolds

While sitting in the teacher's lounge one day with several colleagues, the subject of menopause comes up again. Because many of us are in our forties and fifties, the discussion becomes lively over the fact that we are beginning to feel like couch potatoes and not feeling challenged anymore. We all agree, that with our children grown and independent, this would be a great time to try something new.

Many of us remember that our mothers slowed down, became complacent, and were unwilling to try new things at this age. We don't want to fall into that same trap. Hmmm, what could we do to make our lives more stimulating and exciting?

Later that evening while having dinner with our spouses, Dennis and Don, we listen to their lively conversation about a trip they want to take out West on their motorcycles. Dennis has always been a motorcycle enthusiast, and Don, at the age of 50, transformed himself from a motorcycle wannabe to a real life owner of a shiny new cycle. As they chat about the fun they are going to have on their motorcycles and the sense of freedom of the mountain air, we begin to take an interest in their conversation. Then their discussion turns to Edmonton, Alberta in Canada. We really perk up our ears this time.

Dianne says, "Isn't that where the largest mall in the world is located?"

This might be the adventure we are looking for. We look at each other and Jeanie says, "This *is* the adventure we are looking for!" We begin imagining ourselves in black leather bras getting tattooed. We quickly enter the conversation and tell them to count us in. Despite the look of shock in their eyes, they begin to include us in the planning.

We decide to leave the day after school lets out. This is only one week away and hardly enough time to transform us from teachers into motorcycle mamas. Maybe that just adds to the adventure.

Why do two school teachers agree to ride 4500 miles on a motorcycle? Have you ever left a movie and wondered what it feels like to ride in a hot air balloon, to sail the Caribbean in a small boat, to go white-water rafting, to hike on a mountain trail, to hang glide off a cliff, or for us, to ride a motorcycle? We live in an age where only your imagination, your desires, and of course, your pocketbook limit your ability to make your dreams come true. As we go through menopause, we can decide to follow in the footsteps of our mothers, or we can choose to GO FOR IT!

The rewards of the journey far outweigh the risk of leaving the harbor.

Author Unknown

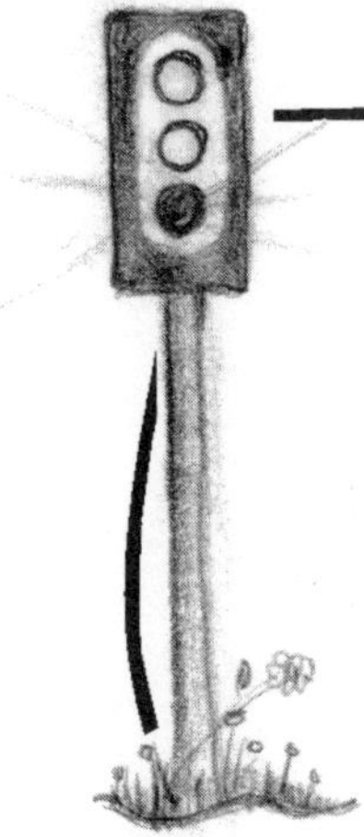

GO FOR IT!

A recent search of the Internet yields thousands of sights offering travel and adventure opportunities from near your home to the far reaches of the globe. Visualize your trip or your adventure while we take you through ours.

The Challenge of Packing

Dianne's Story

It is early afternoon on a Friday, just hours before we leave, and I am getting a headache. Too many preparations to make, too many plans to prepare, too many decisions. Dennis, my husband, and I are in our bedroom packing and have been for some time. With only one small saddlebag to put everything into, I begin to panic. I keep looking at his small pile of clothes out of the corner of my eye, and he keeps checking out my larger pile. I know what he is thinking. Before he can say anything, I quickly bury the curling iron and slide the make-up bag to the bottom of the pile where they will not be seen.

Then I go into the closet and take a very large, very warm, quilted terry cloth robe and place it prominently on top of the pile. At the very instant the robe hits the pile, I hear a desperate, "No, way! Uh-ah!" from my husband. I teasingly argue how nice it would be to have the robe, but then I reluctantly give it up. I know the robe would never fit, but I worry giving it up might require sacrificing something else that I really want to bring—like my make-up and curling iron. Perchance I might be packing too many things. To reaffirm my choices, I call up Jeanie to see what she is packing.

"Three shirts and two pairs of jeans," she says.

Three shirts and two pairs of jeans? How am I to keep up my image with three shirts and two pairs of jeans stuffed into a tiny duffel bag?

Reluctantly, I march back to my pile and start to sweat as I weed out the things I have to leave behind.

We find this idea of selectivity to be true in our own lives. The season of menopause is a time to sort out what we want to keep, what we need to leave behind. It is tough. We all have dreams unfulfilled, old guilts, and clutter that weigh us down.

Our life is frittered away by detail…
Simplify, simplify.

Henry David Thoreau

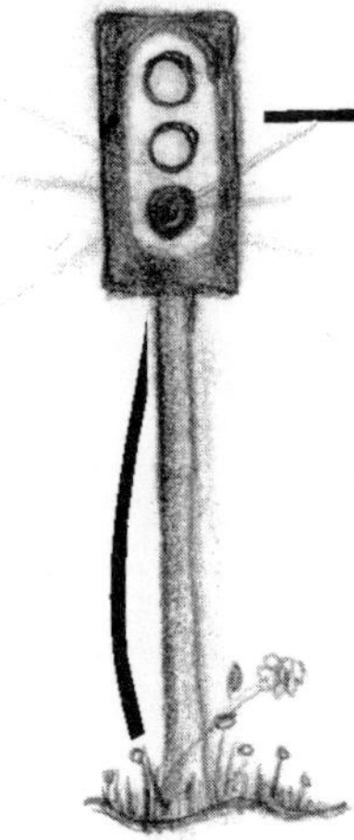

GO FOR IT!

Unclutter your calendar by finding things you don't need to do anymore. Fill it up with things you want to do. At this age it's often okay to put off 'til tomorrow what could be done today.

Unclutter your mind by taking a relaxation class or simply a bubble bath.

Unclutter your life and quit collecting. (You know what we mean.)

What's cluttering your life??

Ooh, Deja Vu

Jeanie's Story

"Who is on the phone?" asks Don.

"That's Dianne," I answer. "She wants to know what I am packing.

She says she's bringing her robe. Do you think I need my robe?"

Before he has a chance to utter a negation, our children, Kara and Mark, enter the room. They had come over several hours earlier to find out what they need to do to maintain the house while we are away. They are waiting to say goodbye and see us off.

"Did you make up that list of places that you'll be staying at?" Mark asks us.

"Yep, it's on the kitchen table."

They stand silent and watch us finish packing. It seems as though they have something to say but don't know exactly how to begin. The silence continues until…

"You know that sometimes cars can't see you very well?"

"Yeah, we know."

"Do you have enough rain gear?"

"Yep."

The barrage of concerned questions continues to flood the afternoon until finally we stuff the last of the all-too-small bags into the corners and crevices of the motorcycles. When we finally hop on our cycles and are ready to leave, the last image we see is of our adult children on the front steps waving good-bye and yelling that we should be careful and call them soon to let them know how we are doing.

The familiarity of the whole scene is almost eerie. How did they master the game of 101 questions? When did they develop such concern? Ooh, deja vu!

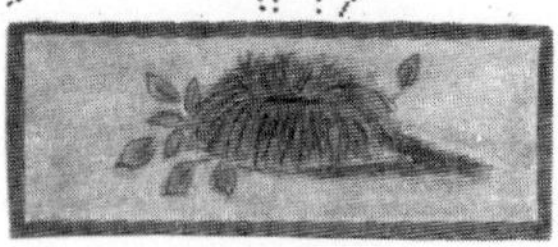

Our nest is now empty, and our lives are changing. We are entering a new season. It is a season of freedom and adventure and satisfaction and fulfillment. Freedom at last is ours. Those children on the front steps waving good-bye are no longer dependent on us.

There is nothing more liberating than age.

Liz Carpenter

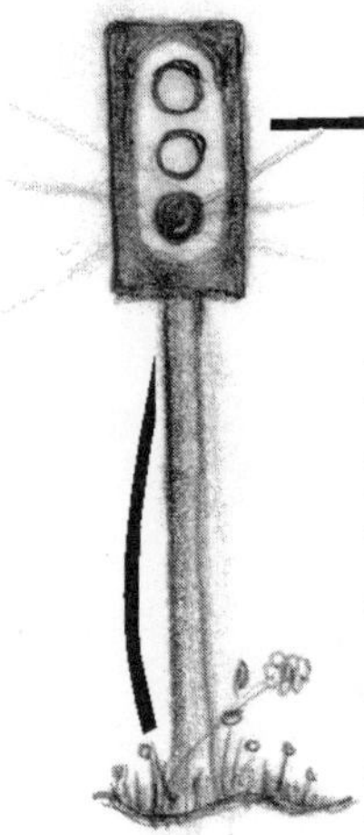

GO FOR IT!

Embrace your new freedom and have a glass of Italian wine with a candle-light dinner tonight.

Go to an Italian restaurant and have a glass of Italian wine with dinner.

Go to Italy and have a glass of local Italian wine…

What are the opportunities that your new freedom provides for you?

The Beginning

As we finally begin this adventure, our minds are drawn to the last minute panic of have we forgotten anything? We are instantly reassured by our husbands that we have filled every available square inch of space the motorcycles have to offer and could not possibly have forgotten a thing.

As we leave the city, the sky quickly begins to darken. We distinctly remember the man in front of a weather map saying with little chance of rain, "Enjoy your day." Soon big drops begin splashing on the pavement below, and we quickly get off the road to slip into our rain gear. With the rain pouring down, we discover our raingear is at the very bottom of the luggage carriers. After unpacking and repacking everything, we hastily pull on the gear, and we hear that distinctive sound of material tearing, followed by Dianne turning around, bending over and asking, "How bad is it?"

"Not bad," we lie, as we hastily sit on the now very wet seats ready to move on. The rain continues, and Dianne begins to discover the full extent of the problem below.

With water continuing to run where it should not, Dianne identifies another glitch in our planning. We have forgotten to develop a universally understood set of hand signals between motorcycles to account for the eventualities of life with menopausal women. How can we let each other know that we quickly need a rest stop and need it now? Some obvious charades get the message across, and we find ourselves at a gas station with a convenience store. While we make use of the convenience, the guys fill the bikes with gas. As we return, we see there are now several other motorcyclists stopped at the station as well. Our husbands have already engaged the riders in conversation. Through their hand gestures, after all we had just played charades, it seems obvious the topic of conversation is the hole in Dianne's rain pants.

We rejoin the group just as one of the other riders holds out a roll of duct tape, joking that this will add to its 101 uses. Dianne bends over and Jeanie awkwardly applies numerous layers of the gray tape. A distinctive flash of a camera records the event. As comments such as, "If only your students could see you now," abound, we all begin to laugh. Not one of us could have planned for this eventuality.

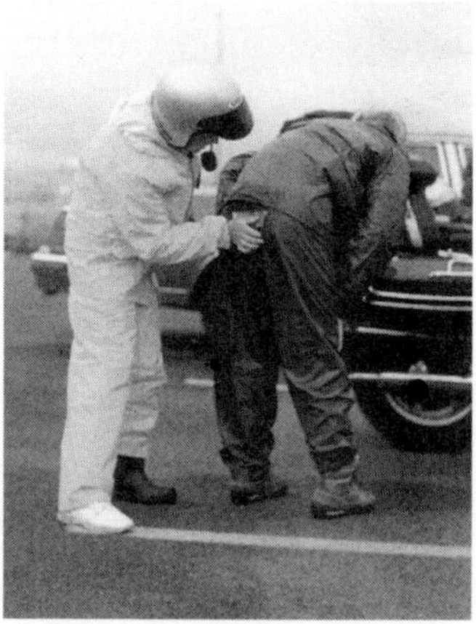

Many of you are beginning your trip through menopause while we are beginning our trip on motorcycles. We put much planning into our motorcycle trip, and we all try to imagine what the adventure might be like. Throughout the trip, from the beginning to the end, we find how little one can prepare for something that is unknown. There is always a glitch or something unexpected around the next turn in the road. The same is true in our lives. We imagine what our lives might be like as we age, but we never truly know how it feels until we reach that time. Like our motorcycle trip, we plan carefully before, plan as we go, and count on the friends we meet along the way. While some aspects of menopause and some aspects of motorcycling have a degree of unpleasantness, with humor and a positive attitude, you can enjoy the ride.

We're only young once, but with humor, we can be immature forever.

Art Gliner

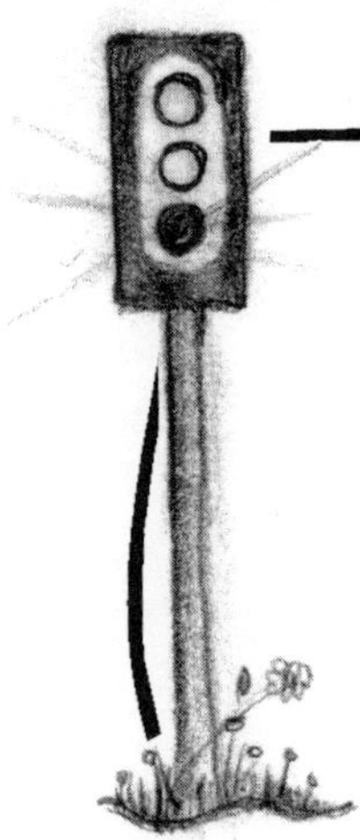

GO FOR IT!

Do something new for the first time.

Explore someone else's interests.

Buy a roll of duct tape.

These are a Few of Our Favorite Things

One of the best things about a motorcycle is being able to experience the outdoors first hand, to be a step closer to nature. Riding through the vast openness ignites the senses, brings the smells, sounds, and sights nearer to you than you ever imagined, sometimes closer than you wish. The scenery floating by appears so intimate that you feel you can reach out and touch it.

The sweetness of newly mown hay, the fragrance of the wildflowers, the freshness of the air after the early morning rain, and the intense smell of mountain pines delights the nose. You also experience the less desirable, pungent smells of pigs, cattle, and an occasional dead skunk making everything more real and alive. While the air rushes past, you feel raindrops splashing on your face as distant thunder echoes through the hillsides. You can, with an unobstructed clearness, see the mountains, the prairies, the winding roads, the grass, and the colors of summer strewn about, as if painted by some unrevealed artist.

One time, riding through mountains, we hear the shrill, piercing call of a hawk as it flies down so close to us that we fear it is we—and not the rodent along the road—that it is

after. These sights, sounds, and smells are as endless as the roads that stretch throughout our great land and are just a few of our favorite things while riding on our motorcycles.

Not just on vacations, but everyday, we try to take notice of little things and appreciate them for what they are. God doesn't want us, no matter what our age, to miss the blossoming flowers, the golden leaves in the fall, the feel of a refreshing rain, or the joy of a child's smile. Each image becomes a memory of our own to treasure. Focusing on wonder and beauty lessens a tendency to dwell on middle age maladies.

Everything has beauty, but not everyone sees it.

Confucius

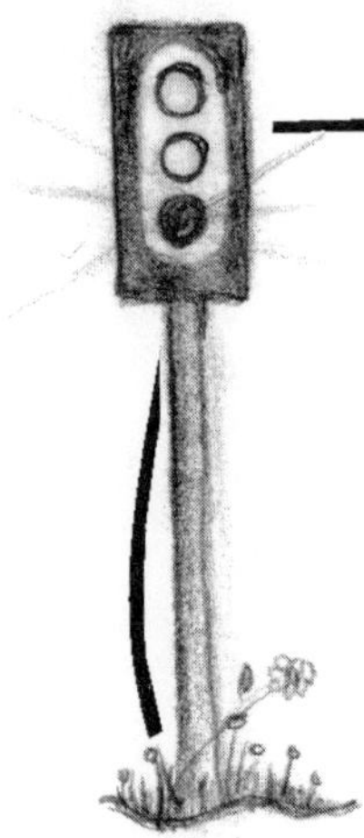

GO FOR IT!

Take a slow, quiet walk in the woods and *really* look at the trees, flowers, birds and plants. God talks to us through nature. Shhhhhhhh—listen.

On a warm sunny day, instead of gathering your family around the dinner table, how about grabbing a picnic basket and meeting at a nearby beach or park?

A Birdhouse in Hand is Worth...

One of our favorite things to do on a trip is to stop in the small towns and explore their uniqueness—the different avenues, houses, coffee shops, restaurants and stores. Each town, small or large, is distinct in its own way. A lazy day in a small Canadian town finds us strolling through the European-like cobblestone streets—talking, window shopping, looking for nothing in particular, enjoying it all.

We stop at an interesting boutique and Jeanie nudges me inside. Our husbands stroll onward and find an empty bench on the corner. Inside, the potpourri-scented store is marvelous, an eclectic mélange of arts and crafts, memorabilia and keepsakes. For several days we have been looking for souvenirs, something to take home, something to remember the trip by. Neither of us has a notion of what we are looking for, but we walk through the aisles nonetheless, guided by intuition and our dedication to finding the perfect souvenir. Around the corner and down the last aisle Jeanie finds it.

She stands in front of a beautiful five-foot high birdhouse with a gaze in her eyes that tells me she has been looking for this exact birdhouse for years; she seems impervious to the fact that we are traveling by motorcycle. I remind her. Her

eyes drop, and we begin to laugh. We laugh together, picturing the birdhouse strapped upon her back cruising down the highways at sixty miles an hour, a flock of birds chasing and circling overhead.

The birdhouse remains in the potpourri-scented store in the small Canadian town and, a few hours later, Jeanie's disappointment fades.

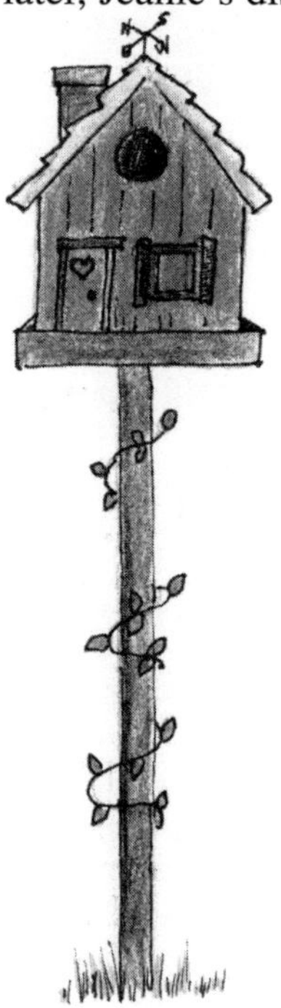

Looking back on our own lives, we are convinced that it is not always the material things that we buy that lead to our happiness, but rather the memories that we gather by spending time with our family and friends.

The best and most beautiful things in the world cannot be seen nor touched... but are felt by the heart.

Helen Keller

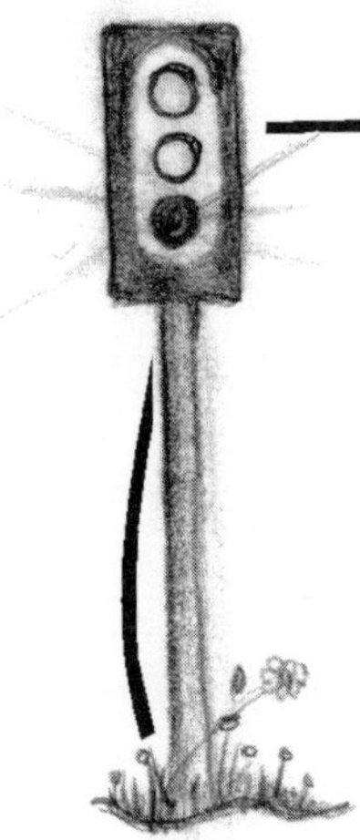

GO FOR IT!

Look up a friend that you haven't seen for over twenty years and reconnect.

Try hosting a slumber party for some old friends.

With a relative, dig out some old photographs and create a new album together sharing lost memories.

Plan a family reunion this yeat.

The Five by Six Motel

Driving endless hours through the flatlands and farms of Saskatchewan makes our road trip through North Dakota seem like a scenic masterpiece. Saskatchewan is, of course, beautiful in its own right, but after hour upon hour it wearies the most patient of minds. By the time we stop for the night, we are extremely tired and looking forward to a long, hot shower and some relaxation.

After unsuccessfully trying to find rooms at many motels, a helpful clerk explains the reason the motels in town are so full is because it's the big annual rodeo. The next city with the likelihood of having rooms is an unbearable 100 miles away. He kindly lends us the Yellow Pages and the use of his telephone. We scroll through the listings calling all of the motels in order and getting the same rejections. Our fingers finally point to a single line in some very fine print, the only motel that we have not yet tried: the 506 Motel. We call. Two rooms. The *last* two rooms in town. Two rooms at the 506 Motel!

We thank the helpful clerk, hop on our motorcycles heading toward the motel intent on getting those rooms. If we don't get those rooms, the park benches along the way might be our only choice for the night.

We get to the motel. We rush into the lobby. While waiting at the desk for service, two other groups join in line behind us. While we are enjoying the security of being in front of the other customers, Dianne calmly asks the clerk, "May we see the rooms before we reserve them, please?" Three jaws drop at the mention of the question, while four others in the line behind become unexpectedly more attentive. Shrinking back from the dirty looks, Dianne retracts her comment telling the clerk that we are sure the rooms will be acceptable and that we will take them.

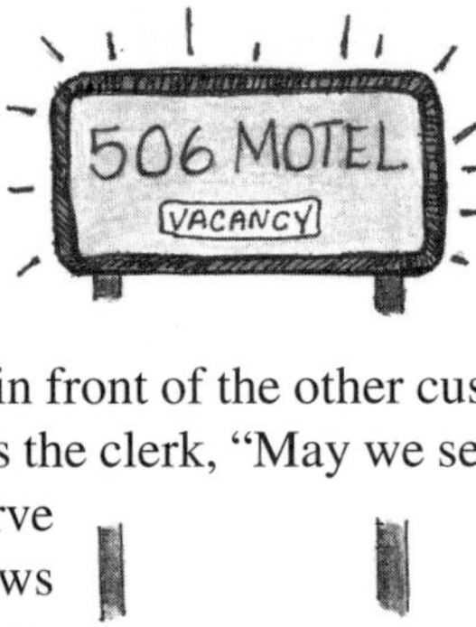

After getting the keys, we soon discover the irony in the name 506. The rooms' dimensions are little more than five feet by six feet.

After showering and getting dressed on the bed (there isn't enough floor space), we head out for dinner. Sitting around the table at dinner, we have a good laugh thinking about our tight confinements in the 506. We are fortunate to have clean sheets and a roof, albeit a small roof, over our heads for the night.

Some of our answers to problems often come in a different manner then we expect or desire—perhaps in fine print at the end of a list. Facing new problems of menopause often require creative new solutions such as... *What do you do with insomnia and hot flashes?* We need to keep searching for answers, but also develop an attitude of acceptance and know that this, too, shall pass.

There are two ways of meeting difficulties: you alter the difficulties or you alter yourself to meet them.

Phyllis Bottome

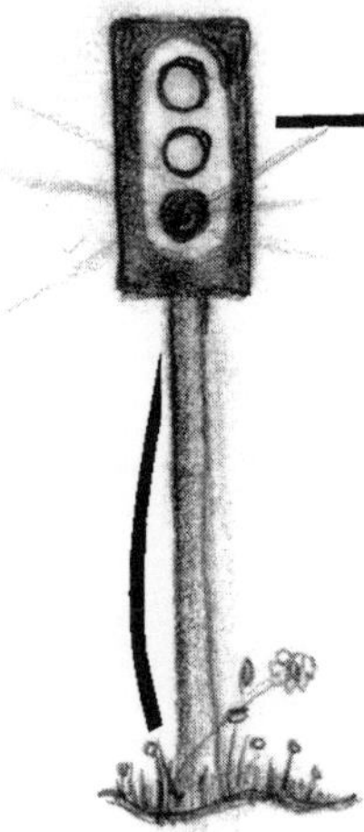

GO FOR IT!

Insomnia?

Rather than fighting sleep, try listening to soothing music or a relaxation tape.

Calm yourself with the visual imagery of a beautiful sunset, a quiet beach, or a special place of relaxation just for you.

Hot flashes?

When having a hot flash, think of it as having your own private summer, and layer those clothes so you can rip them off!

Everybody Needs a Little KFC

We have been moving at a steady pace all day, trekking through Saskatchewan and Alberta, trying to make it past Regina before nightfall. We are told that tomorrow there is a festival in Calgary that will create a major traffic jam, so we drive on throughout the day as our bodies become weary. We had planned several days for just riding, and on this day, we now had to make it further than we had initially planned. We are tired, our hair is frazzled and the greasy sunblock on our faces has been attracting dust, dirt, and bugs from the road for more than eight hours.

Late in the afternoon, we pull over in a small town for gas and to take a break. We are plenty tired but know that we have at least two more hours if we are to get close to Regina. We discuss stopping short and checking in for the night, but in the end we decide that it would be best if we push on. The feeling of refreshment is only temporary and we begin to rethink our decision to proceed. Forty-five minutes after we decide to go on, we stop once again.

All of us are tired, and none of us feel like pushing it any further. We don't like stopping short of our goal but feel it is the best thing to do under the circumstances. We check into a nice motel in a wayside town. After settling in, we go down the street and pick up some Kentucky Fried Chicken for dinner and bring it back to the motel where we enjoy a pleasant picnic next to the swimming pool. After eating and swimming, we stretch out on the lawn chairs relaxing, watching the sun dip behind the hills on the horizon. It feels terrific to be off the bikes and to relax at the pool. As we sit there, we take out the map and discuss an alternative route to get past Calgary. The benefits from stopping short of our goal seem well worth it to all of us.

Many women at this age have had goals and now realize that they may need to alter those goals. Reaching those objectives may be too difficult, so we need common sense and wisdom to accept a change in our plans.

Have two goals: Wisdom—that is, knowing and doing right—and common sense. Don't let them slip away, for they fill you with living energy, and are a feather in your cap.

Proverbs 3: 21-22, Living Bible

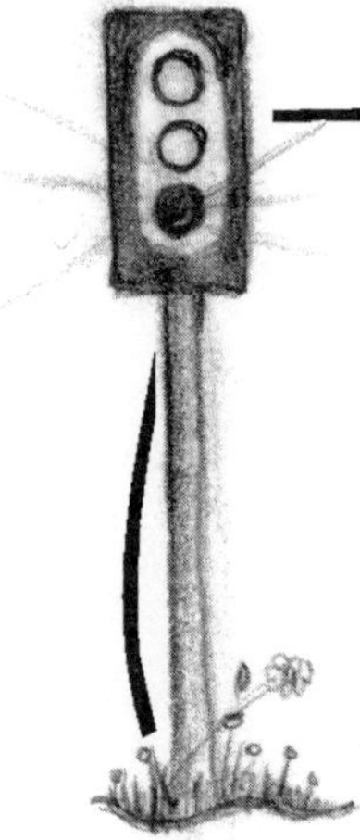

GO FOR IT!

Find a new way of pursuing an old, unfulfilled interest.

If you didn't get your dream job, how about volunteering in that area? (We are hoping you did not dream about being a surgeon.)

What was your dream or interest and how can you alter it to still make it come true?

Detours

By the fourth day of our trip, we near Edmonton, Canada. Living in Minnesota, it is hard to imagine anything grander (when it comes to shopping) than our own Mall of America. However, we are headed this day, under thickening gray skies, to the largest mall in the world—the West Edmonton MegaMall. As we near it, however, brilliant strokes of lightning pulse through the darkening afternoon sky, and rain, unannounced, begins rapidly pelting against our raingear and helmets. The road becomes slick, and we see a lightning bolt pierce the ground in the distance. Our shopping ambition becomes dampened and all four of us readily agree to wait this one out.

We stop in a small Canadian town and motor to the only open restaurant. A little disappointed and very wet, we enter the Greek restaurant and become unmovable patrons for the next six hours as the storm billows in strength, blowing blankets of rain across this small Canadian town, refusing our requests to move out of our path.

We really only have two choices at this point: we can either complain about the weather and the missed shopping opportunity, or we can give in to circumstances, relax and enjoy the day that has been handed us. One certainty in life, we have learned, is that no matter how much control you may feel at a particular moment, the next instant can prove this stability false.

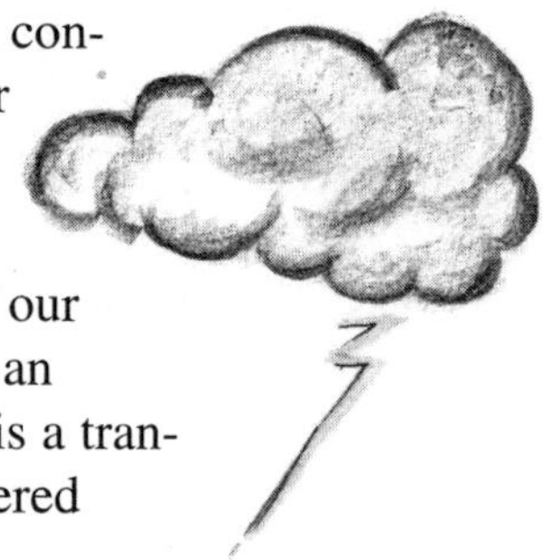

We take off our raingear, kick off our boots, eat gyros, kabobs, and down an unknown quantity of coffee. There is a tranquility in this cozy restaurant, sheltered from a tumultuous storm, and it affords us an opportunity to enjoy each other's company and laugh away the stormy afternoon. At the end of the afternoon, as shades of blue begin to crawl over the mountains, and the rain subsides to a slight drizzle, we hop on our cycles and head onward. Unexpected serendipity.

Looking back, this detour offered unexpected memories, and the time spent in the Greek restaurant in the small Canadian town will always be cherished. Likewise, menopause feels like a detour in our lives that can also bring about some benefits. Don't miss out on a blessing because it isn't packaged the way you expect.

Change is not made without inconvenience, even from worse to better.

R. Hooker

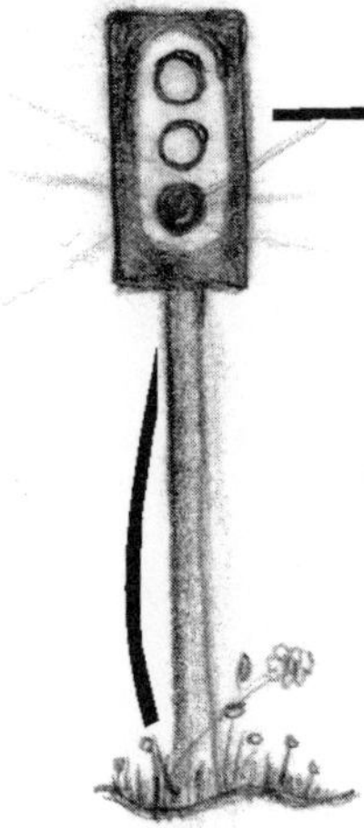

GO FOR IT!

Watch and wait for the benefits coming your way.

Under Where?

Living out of a duffel bag that is wrapped in a plastic garbage bag and eventually stuffed into a saddlebag, forces us to be selective in choosing what we bring with us. With a limited supply of clothes along, we need to stop at a Laundromat every few days.

One day we stop in Banff at a small Laundromat that is huddled between larger shops on a busy town street. It is an old building, and the striped awning hangs limply over the large windowpane that faces the street. LAUNDROMAT is spelled out in wide ragged painted red letters on top of the window.

We con our husbands into starting the laundry, assuring them that we will be back soon to give them a break. They're pretty nice guys, but laundry isn't one of their favorite things to do. They say it ruins their motorcycle image.

The variety of shops immediately turns our attention toward shopping, and we are soon off exploring the different stores, being unaware of time passing and forgetting our obligations at the Laundromat. It isn't until a couple hours later, as we pass a men's department store, that we remember our husbands.

As we hurriedly walk back down the busy street toward the Laundromat, we feel a twinge of guilt and wonder how the motorcycle men are doing. As we approach them, however, our guilt turns to amusement as we watch our husbands, at the folding board in front of the large window that looks out to the busy street, folding up our underwear into neat little piles. We have *definitely* shattered their motorcycle image.

With a duffel bag full of clean clothes, we are able to start the next day feeling refreshed for the adventure that awaits us. Like our clothes, we need to routinely "launder" our souls by taking time out of our busy schedules to initiate our own spiritual cleansing. Taking time for ourselves to pause and refresh helps spin a new perspective on our lives and offers that renewed energy that we need to meet each new day.

Put your ear down close to your soul and listen hard.

Anne Sexton

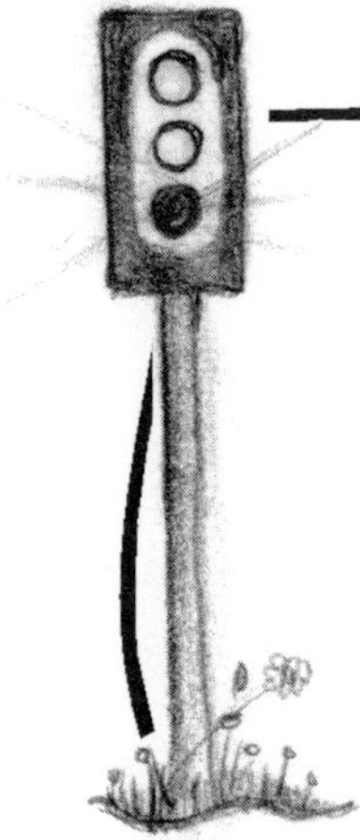

GO FOR IT!

Daily find your own quiet place to pray or meditate.

Whenever you can, curl up with your comfy robe, grab a cup of hot chocolate, and read an inspiring book. Hmm… How about *Motorcycling Through Menopause*?

Where is your favorite place to find your spirit?

Lake Louise

We plan on visiting Lake Louise in the morning as we leave Banff, Canada, and continue on our journey. We have all been there before and remember it being one of the most beautiful sights in nature that we have ever seen. We are all excited about revisiting. The day we choose, however, is awful.

We set out early in the morning. The sky is a damp gray. Fog etches its way out of the forests and onto the highway licking at our legs as we drive along, forcing the green foliage at the side of the road to cower in despair. The pines, normally stately and grand, droop with bad posture, their arms hanging low. Birds fly elsewhere, and all other wildlife stay in their homes, waiting for the dreary day to leave. In fact, the only ones that seem to be really enjoying the day are the gnats (not to be confused with the ones splattered on the windshield) that whiz by us at sixty miles an hour.

We feel disappointment as we park our motorcycles and start to walk down the trail that leads to Lake Louise. We had earlier envisioned that perfect day. As we walk further down the trail, we witness something spectacular. The sun, which has been meek and hidden all morning, forces its way through the dissipating clouds. The trail, still deep in the

woods, lights up with a golden hue that spreads through the mass of huddled pine needles. When the trail ends and opens up, we see Lake Louise, in all its splendid glory, welcoming the sun and the new day. The dreariness of the day unfolds before our eyes, and we marvel all morning at this wonder of nature, our spirits soaring.

Just as rain, sleet and wind are not permanent emblems of the summer season, disappointment, depression and despair are not permanent emblems of this season of life. They never need to be anyway. Since we don't call summer 'the season of rain' we should think of this season of life with no less regard. Life is a gift, age is a treasure.

Keep your face to the sunshine...and you cannot see the shadows.

Helen Keller

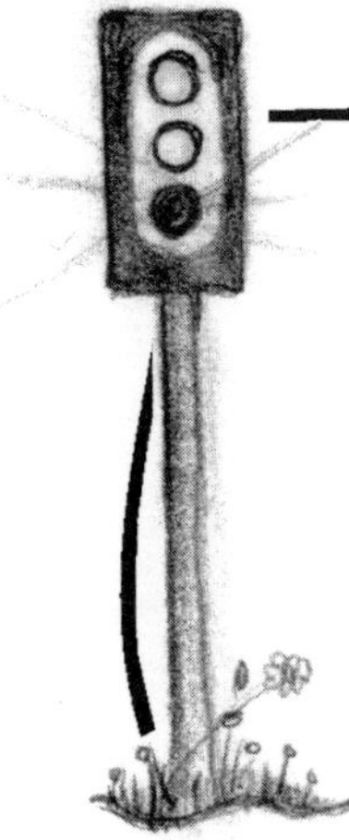

GO FOR IT!

Keep a Gratitude Journal noting the positive things occurring in your life, and write about them each day. If the journal is still empty after a year, seek professional help.

When you are fretting about something, try to remember what you were fretting about one year ago today.

Bring sunshine into someone's life by remembering to not only tell those you love how you feel, but give them a hug as well.

Who needs to hear loving words from you today?

The Moment of Now

Dennis Tunes Out Dianne

"Slow down around that curve!" I speak into the headset.

"Uh hah," comes the reply.

"Be careful when we pass that semi!" I speak into the headset.

"Uh hah."

"Honey, did you turn off the headset?" There is no reply.

Dennis shakes his helmet and his voice comes through my earphones, "No, I didn't turn off the headset."

Sometimes I wonder, though, if he did turn it off after talking straight for a half-hour or so and getting only that occasional, "Uh hah" response.

I am, however, after riding for several straight days, beginning to understand what he is thinking, or rather feeling, even in the absence of communication. The motorcycle becomes a medium of meditation. The endless hours of the murmuring wind meshed with the soft humming of the machine create an inescapable feeling of tranquility. What motorcycling is about is being in the now. For the specific moment, we become part of this vast and endless nature—breathing in the wetness of the Canadian Rockies, tasting the dryness of a desert, cowering in the cold wind, or tracing the brilliance of the sun on a perfect day.

As the trip goes on, we will discover these moments of perfection. For an instant, we peer into the future riding down those country roads looking ahead, but in that same instant, the past breezes by at 60 mph. And the motorcycle, for each single moment, is trapped between this past and this future and sometimes the moment becomes perfect.

As I begin to understand the perfection of these moments, I know why my husband doesn't want to talk all the time, and in fact, I stop warning him of things to come. Well…except for the mountain goats that jump out of nowhere and scare both of us half to death. But then the response to that one is much more than his usual, "Uh hah!"

It seems our husbands can sometimes only concentrate on one thing at a time. While it's frustrating when they ignore us, maybe we should learn from their example. This season of life gives us a perfect time to absorb special moments while having the wisdom to distinguish between the "Uh hah's" and the mountain goats in the road of life.

There is a certain sweetness in being what one is now... So appreciative, so enjoying, so grateful for what has been, and for what is now.

Bernard Berenson

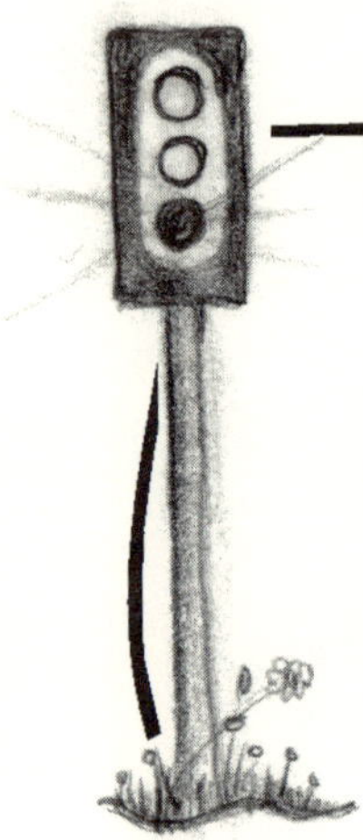

GO FOR IT!

Take time for yourself. Spend an hour in the park, an hour at the mall, or an hour napping on the couch.

Reserve tickets for an upcoming concert. You will enjoy the now, then.

One Too Many

Every morning we try to hear the weather forecast for the day so we can dress accordingly. Riding on the motorcycles can prove to be cool even on a warm day. Dianne, who does anything she can to stay warm, often finds herself overdressing.

One morning, after watching the news that predicted a cool day, the three of us wait patiently for Dianne as she finishes layering on every article of clothing that she brought with her—long johns, turtlenecks, long sleeved shirts, wool sweater, vest, scarf, an insulated-lined jacket, and on this particular day, the bright yellow rubberized rain suit.

Walking out of her motel room, helmet on, every inch of her body covered, she declares to us in a muffled voice from under her scarf, "I'm not gonna be cold today!" The sight of her determination to stay warm makes us all laugh inside as we give her a sarcastic nod of agreement. The three of us are dressed in half of what she is wearing and we know that she will soon be too warm once we get going.

The first few minutes of the ride are actually cold, and I often look over at Dianne whose smile tells me she is comfortably warm. I start second-guessing myself for not putting on more layers. But then the sun, which has been stuck in the

East under a cloud, comes out, and it starts to get warm. Real warm. I look over at Dianne and give her a big smile. I can tell she is now the one who is uncomfortable.

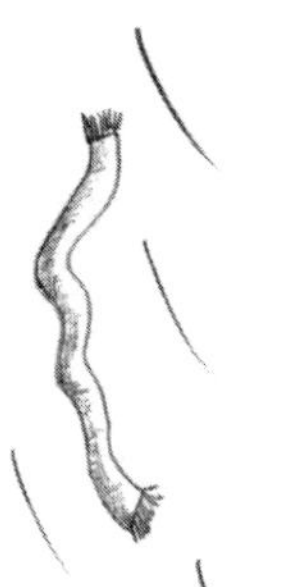

We ride on for quite awhile under the warming sun until Dianne and Dennis suddenly turn down a deserted country road. By the time we stop and turn around to see what's up, Dianne is peeling off the layers as fast as she can and dumping her clothes in a steamy pile by the side of the road. The three of us knowingly smirk at each other.

As menopausal women, we tend to become more cautious and stressed in life. We have developed our own layers of protection against change, defending ourselves against any unpleasantness. Some of these layers are healthy and normal, but we should remember not to overdo. Don't put on that ole' winter jacket for a summer stroll.

And we shed so many other layers of ourselves as we become closer to our own core.

Ellen Sue Stem

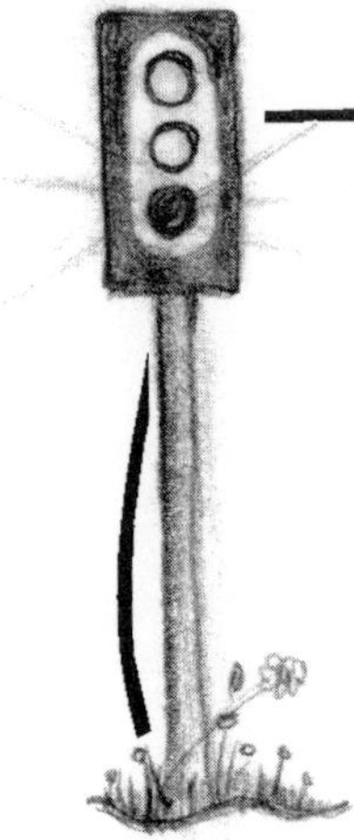

GO FOR IT!

Take off the layers of protection against change by…

- Not being afraid of getting lost. Take out a map and find your way to a new place for lunch. If you are like us, though, you may want to give yourself a few extra minutes just in case.
- Using this simple idea… add variety to your life by taking different routes to places you have been before. Change can be fun.
- If you've worn the same hairstyle for years, change it.

What layers of protection are weighing you down?

Conquering Our Limitations

Dianne's Hang-up

About a year before we are to leave on our trip, I develop an arrhythmia in my heartbeat. It is a strange and terrifying sensation to have an irregular heartbeat, and a problem that makes me delve into the issue of my mortality. When the arrhythmia first started, it was sporadic and slow, missing a beat only a couple of times a minute. As time went on, it became even more irregular, until it started skipping several times a minute. I have lived my entire life without giving my heartbeat much of a thought, but when it starts skipping and feeling strange, I seem to have no other choice than to constantly dwell upon the irregularity. Apprehensions press through my mind bringing with them a whirlwind of emotions. With clenched teeth, I often wonder which skip might be the final skip.

After a few long months, the doctors, cardiologists and experts finally come upon a diagnosis. They are not exactly sure what it is. They are, however, in agreement that the condition is benign, but because of their ambiguous diagnosis, my fears only partially subside.

It is with the doctor's approval that I agree to the motorcycle trip. I feel fine and healthy most of the time, although during periods where the heart beats irregularly, my anxiety level increases. Such is the case during this particular morning as we continue on with our journey into Colorado. As we prepare to climb Mount Evans, I wonder how will my heart react to high altitudes? Does the doctor who endorsed this trip for me really know it is safe?

As we begin our ascent of Mount Evans, which is one of the highest paved roads in the country, my anxiety begins to soar. As we climb the steeply paved roads, making hairpin turns, passing cars around winding corners, emerging above the tree lines, my adrenaline is pumping, and I can feel my heart pounding. When we finally reach the top, we cut the engines and the quietness of the mountain fills our ringing ears. Birds soar, diving in the brilliant blue sky as the sun sits cradled between two mountains. On top of our mountain, in the high altitude, I stand silently, facing the sun, feeling alive as my fear and anxiety disappear.

Jeanie's Hang-up

I do not care much for tightly enclosed spaces. In fact, I hate them. Ever since I was young these claustrophobic fears get the best of me. Being on a motorcycle, I find, is the antithesis of claustrophobia. The endless miles of eternal highways ahead, open wilderness everywhere, the sky outlining massive depth, and fresh air all around—breathing in and out the openness of the outside. Yes, motorcycling is the opposite of being in a tightly confined space. I do not think about my claustrophobic fears on a motorcycle trip. I do not think of it until we reach Mesa Verde National Park in Colorado.

I have always been interested in the history of the Anasazi, and I relish the chance to take a tour of their cliff dwellings when we reach the National Park. We choose an especially interesting tour. When the tour begins, we are told the specifics of what it will entail.

"We do *what?*" I ask the tour guide, sounding rather agitated.

"Well," he repeats, "then we go through a small cave that leads to their dwellings."

Panic rises, lighting my skin on fire, forcing small beads of sweat to trickle down my forehead as I think about the expedition. I balk at the thought and almost walk off. I may have, had the others not been there giving disapproving faces at my subtle signs of possible departure. I choose to go on.

First, we climb a sixty-foot ladder, which, since I'm not afraid of heights, is done with ease. Then comes the cave. It is tiny. Yes, it is very tiny.

The tour guide goes through first. I am nervous and afraid, and it is in this state of fear that I volunteer to go first in the group. Crouching on my hands and knees, dirt spilling over my fingertips, I scoot through that small dark and dusty cave to the opening on the other side. The tour guide knows of my claustrophobia (I have been mentioning it casually several times) and commends me on getting through, adding that it is the fastest time ever recorded that anyone has made it through the cave. Being on the high cliff, in the middle of their dwellings, hearing of how the Anasazi lived, is a fantastic experience that I could have easily missed.

Fears and apprehensions have a way of affecting our minds—especially at this age—and this may result in choices that are different from the ones that we desire. If we will something, and are capable of doing it, we should let our fears and apprehensions serve only a secondary role. We need to put them behind us and move ahead.

We gain strength and courage, and confidence by each experience in which we really stop to look fear in the face… we must do that which we think we cannot.

Eleanor Roosevelt

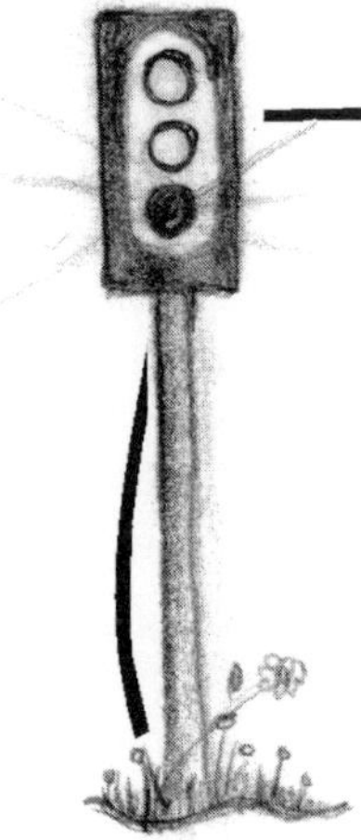

GO FOR IT!

Don't be afraid to:

Take a moment to identify your fear and ask yourself:

Is it rational?
Is it limiting me?
What can I do about it?

Strip yourself of your inhibitions and enjoy those activities that you know you can do if you try.

Helmet Hair

One of the most troublesome parts of the motorcycle trip is the condition we call helmet hair. Helmet hair is the immediate and irreversible result of what the helmet does to the hair. There are, of course, different levels of progression of helmet hair—depending on the length of time the helmet has had to compress the hair into different shapes and sizes. One particularly bad helmet hair day comes after a long, hot and steamy day riding through New Mexico. Stopping at a rest area, we remove our helmets and quickly finger-comb the stringy and limp aftermath.

Jeanie secretly hopes that her own hair does not have as many gray hairs popping out or does not look as bad as Dianne's. Guess what? Dianne is secretly thinking the same thing. When we first look at ourselves in the bathroom mirror, we can't help but start laughing at how disheveled and mussed up our hair has become.

From behind us, we hear an unfamiliar woman's voice saying, "How do you get your hair like that? I've always wanted my hair like that."

"It's easy," Jeanie chuckles, "just wear a helmet all day."

The woman responds as she notices we are traveling by motorcycle, "I didn't realize that is what you were laughing about. It really looks nice on you."

As the woman left, we reexamined our hair in the mirror. It still looked terrible to us, so we decided that maybe the lady mistook our happiness and laughter as outward beauty.

Beauty is from within, and it radiates joy. As we age, we worry about our outward appearances, feeling the loss of our youthful looks. Even though we look in the mirror and see wrinkles and a rounder tummy, we treasure more what we have become. The stranger at the rest area had it right. When we feel happiness on the inside, our outer self radiates that joy. And this is true beauty.

It's about activating sources of internal value and defying the "beauty myth" that constrained us in First Adulthood.

Gail Sheehy

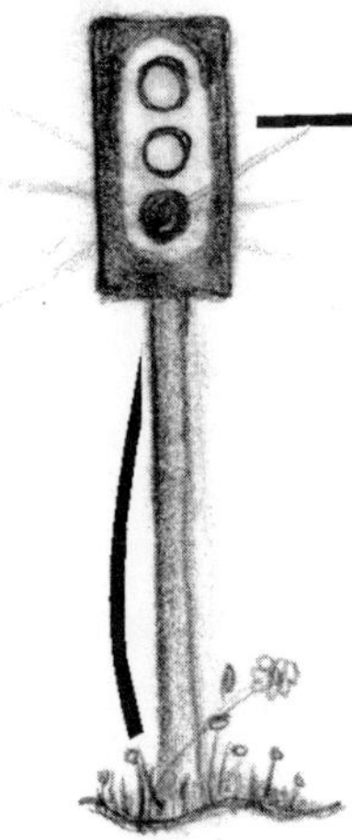

GO FOR IT!

Forget about trying to look like the latest movie star. Just be you! (Ignore this if you happen to be the latest movie star.)

Use those new wrinkle creams and menopausal pimple creams, but spend most of your time smoothing out the wrinkles inside.

What makes you beautiful inside?

Necessitamos Tums!

We stop in Santa Fe at a quaint Mexican restaurant for lunch. We take a table outside, sitting under an umbrella that shades us from the afternoon sun, and become preoccupied with the huge, hot and spicy chicken burritos we have ordered. Gluttonously shoveling in the delicious food, piling mounds of salsa on our chips, we give no thought to the possible effects this food might have on our aging digestive systems.

With a Thanksgiving-Day-like-fullness, we shuffle to the motorcycles, plop ourselves in riding position (with some difficulty) and drive on.

We buzz along under the desert sun. After about an hour of riding, still in a euphoric state of fullness, we each realize that those hot and spicy burritos are waging a *coup d'etat* with our stomachs. Spontaneously, all four of us frantically give the signal for a stop. With the burritos gaining victory, we decide that we are desperately in need of a big

roll of Tums and a bathroom. Having a working definition of "Tum's Stop" in your everyday vernacular is a sure sign of getting older.

"Moderation" might be the word we need to add to our vocabulary at this age. With eating and playing, the body starts speaking to us in ways it didn't before. Listening to our bodies will help all of us prevent so many of those "Tum's Stops."

Be moderate in everything, including moderation.

H Porter

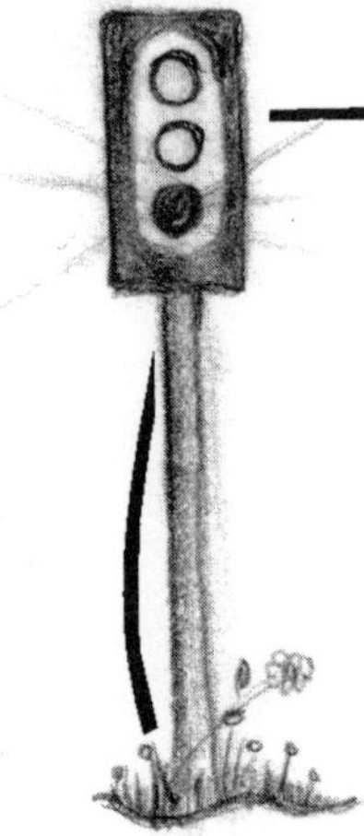

GO FOR IT!

Dance 'til dawn recognizing dawn may come at midnight.

Show that young aerobics instructor that you can keep up…at least through the warm-up anyway.

Once in awhile order that double dutch hot fudge sundae, but keep those Tums handy.

A Similar Experience

With our tanks full of gasoline, our stomachs full of Tums, and after just enough rest, we continue down the highway through New Mexico. Soon, though, we spot clouds ahead, seeping over the mountains and rolling down the wide valley toward us, instilling all with apprehensions. A storm seems inevitable. Towns in New Mexico can be a considerable distance apart, so we decide to head back to the same town from which we had just come. We turn down a different road and head back—driving toward sunshine and blue sky, putting distance between us and the clouded horizon that now fades behind us.

We stop at a Food-N-Fuel and watch the sky for signs of what it might do. Jeanie and I both suffer from what we call a directional deficit, a lifelong deficiency with no known cure. Experts suggest that it might be related to concentrating on topics of conversation rather than where we are going, but we categorically disagree. In layman's terms this means that we often get lost and are prone to lose our sense of direction in critical moments. The peculiar nature of this deficiency is that it is not stifled by age, but rather benefits from it.

In the bathroom at the Food-N-Fuel, Jeanie remarks to me that the bathroom looks remarkably like the one we were in earlier that day. I agree. I had not noticed it before she men-

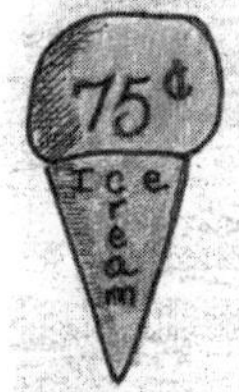

tioned it, but the resemblance is uncanny. Many stores look the same, though, and we remember that the other store was a Food-N-Fuel as well.

Looking for an ice cream cone, Jeanie remarks to me that the snack counter looks identical to the one that we were at before, even the selection of ice cream looks the same. I agree. Exactly like the other one. This seems a little strange.

Then she points to the person behind the counter and says seriously, "They even have the same people working here!" Exactly the same.

"Jeanie," I reply already giggling at having solved the mystery, "We *are* in the same store we just came from."

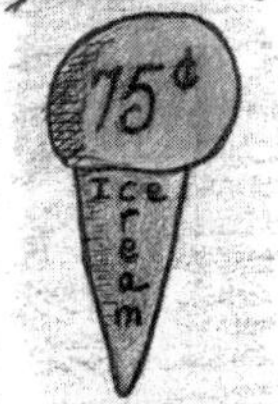

Leaning against the brick wall on the side of the building, trying to eat our ice cream cones, we laugh so much at our mistake that we start to draw glances from passers-by.

The humor of our forgetfulness lasts even to this day. When our memory fades (which is apparently starting to happen), we think back to our incident at the Food-N-Fuel and remember to laugh at ourselves.

If you forget something, don't fret. Forget that you forgot it.

Pearl Swiggum

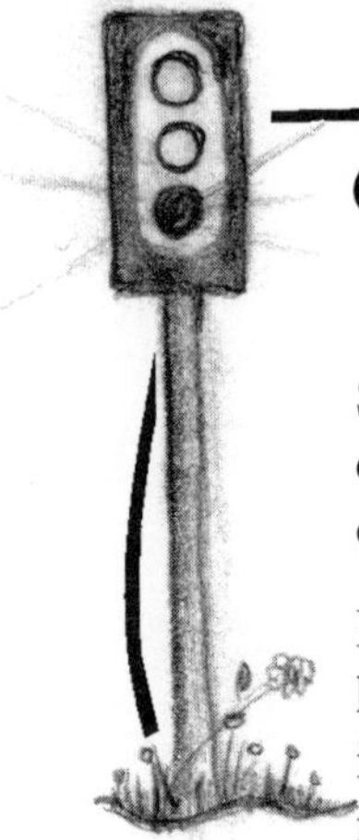

GO FOR IT!

So…you don't remember what you came downstairs for. Laugh at yourself on the way back up.

If you go to the grocery store and come home with everything except the one item you went there for, remember it next time, remember it next time, REMEMBER IT NEXT TIME!

WHEN you forget people's names, just smile.

Some of those forgetful moments become the best stories to tell. We were going to share some of those, but unfortunately…

The Ultimate "Out of Box" Experience

The landscape of South Dakota is familiar to us in our last days of our trip. Our adventures are coming to an end, though we are ready for one more before settling back home. In what appears to be a scene from a post-apocalyptic movie, we find ourselves heading toward the Badlands. The sun splinters off the desert earth, the deep roar of Harleys echoes around the valleys, and black leather and chrome fill the highway in front of us. The sounds of our own motorcycles are drowned by the packs of low rumbling machines that overtake us. We've seen them coming, sparse at first, but now in a fury. We know we are nearing Sturgis, our last adventure before going home.

We don't know what to expect, but we know we want to go. How could we not want to go?

We roll into town behind a large group of bikers. At first glance, the town seems to be a carnival of decadence—people and motorcycles everywhere. Tattooed men. Tattooed women. Black leather jackets, black leather boots, beards, unwashed beards, pierced ears, pierced lips, pierced bellybuttons, pierced everything. Men in full leather outfits, women in hardly anything at all. We are starting to feel a little out of place.

We look at our clean white teacher-type T-shirts. Dianne has chosen this day to wear one with a small red apple and schoolhouse embroidered on it. We laugh when we look at each other (we definitely do not look 'cool'). Soon, though, we find a T-shirt stand where we buy two black Sturgis T-shirts and quickly throw them on.

Now as we wander the streets, feeling like part of the Sturgis crowd, we begin to see the town for what it is. Sure, there is the stereotype, like the one we had when we first arrived, but there is also more. As we talk with different people, we realize that Sturgis is not just one group of people; instead, Sturgis is about motorcycling, and this involves many people from many walks of life, some just like us. All the people we meet are friendly, courteous and enjoyable, and many belong to the same organization as we do—the good old AARP!

As we age and as we watch our parents age, we find that we sometimes become less open-minded and more rigid in our thinking. Many of the people at Sturgis, those that have tattoos, long beards, and leather outfits, do not deserve their stereotypes. What might be true for one person is not true for the next. Once again, we remember the importance of staying open-minded and not to be boxing people in.

To think out of the box is the number-one challenge for enlightened persons.

Mike Vance and Diane Deacon

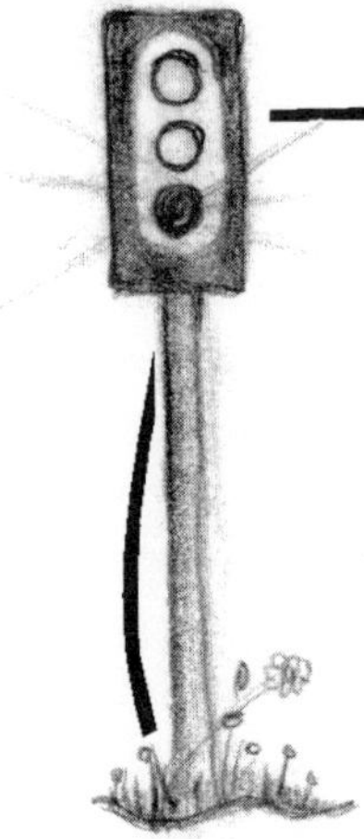

GO FOR IT!

One of the best ways to think out of the box is to crawl into someone else's box.

Volunteer at a soup kitchen. Look for the qualities you have in common. Free soup, too.

To stay young, think young. Hang around with young friends (for as long as they let you).

Conclusion

As we suggest in the prologue, menopause is the beginning of an autumn season—a season of life, which offers excitement, new challenges and rewards.

It is our hope that through this book we are encouraging you to discover the richness of this season in your own lives. It is our wish to motivate you to live out your old dreams and to dream new ones. These dreams don't have to involve motorcycles; they can be done through anything that sparks your interest.

Since our motorcycle adventure, we each have continued to expand and enrich our lives. Dianne has traveled to Guatemala, Turkey, and China. She has also become a breast cancer survivor, an entirely different type of journey, leading to the thought of a new book, *Car Racing Through Cancer.*

Jeanie has taken up sailing, which means conquering her fear of water, and has begun some new artistic endeavors. Together, we are now completing the conclusion of a book we never dreamed possible.

We find that in whatever we do, with the right attitude, the world seems brighter, and our difficulties become smaller. We renew our faith in God each day and continue to feel His spirit lifting us during this beautiful, but complex time of our lives.

Thanks for coming along and joining our ride. Join us in twenty years from now with *Sailing Through Senility* and, later, with our posthumously released *Hitchhiking to Heaven.*

> *Life is either a daring adventure or nothing at all.*
>
> ***Helen Keller***

BLURRED VISION DENIED

My friends tearing down the never-ending highways of life.

The powerful motorcycles throbbing beneath their frail bodies.

My first impression of this blurring image is one of total disbelief!

Flashes of the usual stereotyped motorcyclist rush through my mind:

Motorcycle "gangs," images of the 70's, roaring through small towns, creating fear and chaos.

These are not my friends. No, there must be a mistake—utter impossibility!

Sweet, sophisticated, perfectionist friends of mine.

Proper and well educated, teachers of youth, mothers of idealism.

No, they could not don leather jackets and heavy motorcycle boots.

To cruise the later highways of life atop a powerful and "devilish" machine!

And yet what an exhilarating thrill it must be after such a proper life of doing the expected.

Jenny Adams

About the Authors

Dianne

Age: Undisclosed. Young enough to buy stylish clothes, but old enough to know to buy them a bit bigger.

Job: Teacher. Loves teaching middle school children but remembers having more energy when younger.

Family: Two sons, one stepdaughter. Happy to finally see sons and stepdaughter graduate from college.

Husband: Dennis. A motorcycle enthusiast.

Thoughts: Motocycling. Thought all motorcyclists wore tattoos and leather bras but changes her mind, not her attire, after the trip.

Jeanie

Age: Undisclosed. Young enough to love dining out, but old enough to get a discount.

Job: Teacher. Still looks forward to the first day of teaching elementary school, but is beginning to appreciate the last day even more.

Family: One daughter, one son. Happy to see son and daughter finish college and happily working.

Husband: Don. A former motorcycle "wannabee."

Thoughts: Motorcycling. Thought most motocyclists were "Hell's Angels." Now realize some are fellow AARP members.

A Sampling of Resources for Further Adventures

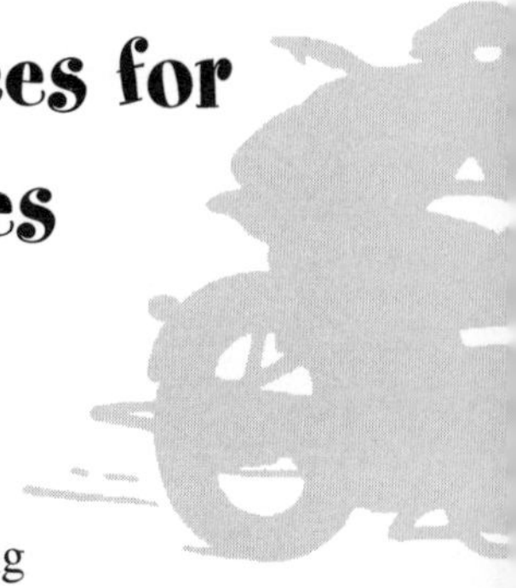

Volunteering Opportunities:

www.volunteermatch.org—Volunteering opportunities in your local area

www.globalvolunteers.com—Service learning travel throughout the world that feeds the soul (1-800-487-1074)

www.habitat.org—A division of Habitat for Humanity that is for women only

Learning/Travel Opportunities:

www.elderhostel.org—"Elderhostel: Adventures in Lifelong Learning" (1-877-426-8056)

www.rightonthemoney.org—"Enriching Your Travel"—Unique and creative travel ideas

Organizations/Clubs:

www.redhatsociety.com—A group for fun-loving 50 year olds found throughout the world

www.friendshipforce.com—An organization for building global goodwill through personal friendships and promoting peace throughout the world

Inspirational Thoughts:

Inspirational Thoughts:

Future Adventures:

Future Adventures: